THE QUICKSAND BOOK

TOMIE DE PAOLA

THE
QUICKSAND
BOOK

HOLIDAY HOUSE · NEW YORK

FOR "STEVEM"
& HIS GRANDMOTHER

Copyright © 1977 by Tomie de Paola
All rights reserved
Printed in the United States of America

Library of Congress Cataloging in Publication Data

De Paola, Thomas Anthony.
The quicksand book.

SUMMARY: Discusses the composition of quicksand
and rescue procedures.
1. Quicksand—Juvenile literature. [1. Quick-
sand] I. Title.
QE471.2.D46   552′.5   76–28762
ISBN 0-8234-0291-6
ISBN 0-8234-0532-X (pbk.)

YOU SEE, WHEN YOU STRUGGLE YOU PUSH MORE
QUICKSAND OUT OF THE WAY AND SINK FASTER.
I'VE NOTICED THAT MOST PEOPLE, IF THEY
STAY CALM, ONLY SINK UP TO THEIR NECKS.
IF YOU HAD FALLEN ON YOUR BACK,
YOU COULD HAVE FLOATED ON TOP OF IT,
THE SAME WAY YOU CAN FLOAT ON THE
GREAT SALT LAKE OR THE DEAD SEA.
BUT IT'S A LITTLE LATE FOR THAT NOW.

DO YOU KNOW WHERE QUICKSAND CAN BE FOUND? NO? WELL, I'LL TELL YOU. THE MOST COMMON FORM OF QUICKSAND IS FOUND ALONG THE SHORES AND IN THE BEDS OF SLOW RIVERS AND STREAMS THAT HAVE UNDERGROUND SPRINGS, JUST LIKE WHERE YOU ARE.

QUICKSAND WILL FORM ALONG SHORES OR UNDER WATER NEAR A BANK.

WATER

QUICKSAND

←SPRINGS→ ←SPRINGS→

ROCK

QUICKSAND WILL SOMETIMES FORM IN MIDSTREAM.

THE SUN BAKES A THIN CRUST ON THE SAND.

ROCK

QUICKSAND

WATER

SPRING

QUICKSAND CAN FORM IN A RIVERBED THAT LOOKS DRY.

THERE IS A THIN CRUST HERE, TOO.
↓

ROCK

QUICKSAND

SPRING

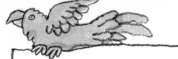

How To Make Your Own Quicksand

1. MAKE A HOLE IN THE BOTTOM OF A PAIL.

2. STICK A HOSE UP THROUGH THE HOLE AND MAKE IT WATERTIGHT.

3. FILL THE PAIL ¾ FULL WITH SAND.

4. PLACE A HEAVY OBJECT ON TOP OF THE SAND. THE OBJECT WILL STAY PUT.

5. TURN ON THE HOSE SO THAT A LITTLE WATER TRICKLES UP THROUGH THE SAND. THE SAND WILL SWELL AND GRAINS WILL PULL APART. WHEN THERE IS ENOUGH WATER TO MAKE THE SAND "QUICK", THE OBJECT WILL SINK.

6. TURN OFF THE WATER. THE SAND WILL SETTLE AND WATER WILL COME TO THE TOP. THE SAND CAN NOW HOLD ANOTHER HEAVY OBJECT. THIS IS BECAUSE THE WATER IS SQUEEZED TOWARD THE TOP, AND THE GRAINS OF SAND AREN'T PULLED APART AS MUCH.